LEADING
◆ WITH ◆
VALUES

8 Common-Sense Leadership Strategies For Bringing Organizational Values To Life

Bud Bilanich

BUD BILANICH

WALKTHETALK.COM

Resources for Personal and Professional Success

Helping Individuals and Organizations Achieve Success
through Values-Based Business Practices

To order additional copies of this handbook, or for information
on other WALK THE TALK® products and services,
contact us at
1.888.822.9255
or visit our website at
www.walkthetalk.com

LEADING WITH VALUES

Inquiries regarding permission for use of the material contained in this book should be
addressed to:

> The WALK THE TALK Company
> 1100 Parker Square, Suite 250
> Flower Mound, Texas 75028
> 972.899.8300

WALK THE TALK books may be purchased for educational, business, or sales promotion use.

WALK THE TALK®, The WALK THE TALK® Company, and WalkTheTalk.com™ are
registered trademarks of Performance Systems Corporation.

Printed in the United States of America
10 9 8 7 6 5 4

ISBN 1-885228-58-9

90000

9 781885 228581

Produced by Steve Ventura
Printed by The Brandt Co.

Introduction

Chances are, your organization has a set of values or operating principles. If yours are similar to those of most businesses, they include a list of items such as: Integrity, Customer Service, Quality, Respect, High Performance, Leadership, and Innovation. Often, these characteristics are followed by additional words that further define them.

You can usually find all of these words in frames or on plaques hanging in peoples' offices and the conference rooms where you work. You, yourself, may have several items – pens, posters, desktop cubes, wallet-sized cards, etc. – as values reminders. All of this is good and well-intended. However, those plaques, cards, posters, and the like are worth next to nothing if people don't live by the words written on them. To have true meaning, beliefs and values must be *lived*, not merely proclaimed.

We all live our lives guided by our own set of personal values. We make decisions based on these principles every day. For example, many people place a very high value on family. These individuals sometimes turn down promotions because of mandatory relocations to different cities – or because of extensive required travel. Other people place a particularly high value on personal integrity. They do things like pointing out to the cashier that he or she has given them change for a twenty dollar bill when, in fact, they paid with a ten. You get the picture.

Organizational values work in the same way. When organizations publish values statements – or otherwise communicate their important beliefs – they are saying to their people, "These are our guiding principles ... what we stand for. If you want to be a part of this business, we expect that you will embrace them and act in a manner consistent with them."

Values "ground" an organization – providing direction for people who find themselves in ambiguous situations. They are guides for decision-making. When employees encounter situations in which they must choose one course of action from a number of different alternatives, they can turn to their organization's values for help. Approached from the context of values, decisions often become less complicated and stress-inducing.

When it comes to organizational values, your job as a leader is critically important. You have a two-fold responsibility. First, you need to make sure that everyone understands what the values are and what they mean. Then, you need to guide people in practicing those values in their day-to-day work lives.

Leaders (that's you!) have to take personal responsibility for their organization's values.

You have to own them and practice them. It's up to you to make sure that your beliefs and principles are more than just words on pieces of paper, plaques on walls, or computer screens on desks. You can do this by asking yourself the questions found on the next page.

■ What can I do to make sure I'm thoroughly familiar with my organization's values and understand how they apply to what we do in my department every day?

■ What can I do to make sure I'm a good role model for my people when it comes to living our values?

■ What can I do to teach my people how to perform their jobs according to our beliefs and guiding principles?

■ What can I do to hold myself and my people accountable for living our organization's values?

■ What obstacles might my people face as they try to live our values? What can I do to remove (or at least minimize) those obstacles?

■ What can I do to reward and encourage team members who demonstrate a true commitment to our values?

■ What can I do to change the behavior of the people who aren't practicing our organization's values?

You'll find the answers to these important questions in the pages that follow. Pay attention to what you read. More importantly, *apply* what you read. Everyone's success is at stake – including your own.

 As you read this book, you'll come across our **Solution Finder!** Visit WalkTheTalk.com where you can immediately access our free tips to help you achieve personal and professional success!

Contents

What's Wrong With This Picture?

Values Horror Story #1

(This story is true. Names have been omitted to protect the guilty.)

After a particularly difficult interaction with a bank teller, a fed-up customer asked to speak with the branch manager to voice his displeasure. While waiting for the manager, he noticed the screen saver on a computer at one of the employee workstations.

The screen saver was devoted to the bank's customer service values. Every few seconds the following messages popped up:

> All of our customers are entitled to fast, accurate, friendly, and courteous service.
>
> Be a Customer Service Professional.
>
> Treat our customers as the most important people in the world – because they are!

After spending a minute or two watching those messages scroll across the screen, the customer was ushered into the manager's office. The ensuing conversation went something like this ...

Customer: I'd like to tell you that I just had a most unpleasant transaction with one of your tellers.

[*The customer then points to the teller and provides a detailed description of the occurrence.*]

Manager: Oh dear. I'll have a talk with her. I'm sorry you had a bad experience. Please accept my sincere apology. Thank you for bringing this situation to my attention.

Customer: I think you *should* talk to her. You know, as I was waiting for you, I was looking at the computer on that desk over there. I can tell you that your teller didn't do *anything* that was on that screen.

Manager [*with a puzzled look on his face*]: I'm sorry, but I'm not sure I understand what you're referring to.

Customer: You know, the stuff on your screen saver about customer service – courtesy, treat customers like they're the most important people in the world ... and so on.

Manager [*smiling with relief*]: Oh, *that*. Now I understand. You'll have to forgive me. They changed all of our screen savers several weeks ago. I've been so busy with new accounts that I haven't had time to review my screen. But I'm sure it's important information. I'll have to take a look.

Customer [*shaking his head*]: You might want to do just that. Have the teller read it, too. And I would suggest doing it sooner than later. If I ever have a bad experience like that again, you will lose my business.

Here's what's wrong with that picture: The bank's headquarters spent a lot of time and money creating screen savers that highlighted their customer service values. But the branch manager didn't know what information was being presented – it was just background noise as far as he was concerned. How in the world could he expect others to pay attention to what he himself ignored? How could he lead by values if he was "too busy" to even read them? The answer to both questions: He couldn't.

Was the manager at fault for not ensuring that everyone, including himself, knew and followed what was on the screen saver? Yes. Was the bank at fault for not developing more effective ways of communicating its key values? Perhaps. Ultimately, however, who's at fault really doesn't matter. What does matter is this:

A key leader wasn't paying attention to his organization's values ... and one of his people was ignoring them altogether. It showed in poor customer service.

Values are nothing more than words on paper (or in this case, a computer screen) unless and until everyone in the organization USES them to guide daily behaviors.

You, and every other leader in the organization, are accountable for ensuring that your people not only *know* the values, but *practice* them as well.

YOU have to assume personal responsibility for making your guiding principles come alive – every day. YOU must be personally accountable for your organization's values.

8 Common-Sense Leadership Strategies For Bringing Organizational Values To Life

1. Develop A Personal Understanding Of Your Organization's Values

2. Be A Values Role Model For Your Employees

3. Communicate Values As Job Expectations

4. Become A Teacher ... By Asking Questions

5. Remove Obstacles To Bringing Values To Life

6. Reward Those Who Live The Values

7. Redirect People Who Aren't Living The Values

8. Never Give In Or Give Up

1 Develop A Personal Understanding Of Your Organization's Values

If you're going to practice values-driven leadership, you need to delve into your organization's values; you need to think about what they really mean to you and your unique leadership situation.

Fact is, if your business' beliefs and principles don't have meaning for you, you won't be able to make them meaningful for the people you lead. Values are just nice words on paper unless people can assign personal meaning to them.

"Sounds great," you say, "but how do I do that?"

Well, it's really not that difficult. All it takes is some thinking and introspection. First, the thinking: Pick one of your organization's values. Read what's written about it, and reflect on your leadership situation. How SPECIFICALLY does that value apply to you and the people in your work group?

Here's an example for clarification:

Many organizations have written (or at least professed) values that have something to do with "customer service." Usually the words associated with a customer service value focus on *external* customers – the people who buy your organization's products or services. Well, the truth of the matter is that very few people in any organization interact directly with external customers. Therefore, it can be easy for leaders – and employees in their departments who don't deal with external customers – to discount the customer service value. "Sure, it's important. But it really doesn't apply to our particular group, right?" Wrong! Customer service is *everyone's* business! All employees have people they work for ... people they serve. Everyone has to be focused on providing top-notch customer service – regardless of whether it's being done for people outside *or* inside the organization.

Good leaders understand the importance of high-quality customer service, and they make it come alive for the people they lead. *Excellent* leaders do that for *all* of their organization's values. You need to analyze and dissect each value, and link it to the functions that you and your people perform. Once that's done, *you're* done ... with the thinking part.

Next comes introspection. Ask yourself, "Does this organizational value mesh with my personal value system? Are there any conflicts between the two?" Customer service is useful as an example here as well.

Ask most people what they value most in life, and you probably won't hear "serving customers." You're more likely to hear things such as: "my family," "my faith," "personal integrity," "keeping my word," and "being a good friend." That's to be expected – it's normal and perfectly okay.

As long as your personal values don't conflict with your organizational values, you're fine. You might not answer "customer service" when somebody asks you what you hold most near and dear. But, if you believe that serving customers is important to the success of your business, you'll likely accept it as one of your job responsibilities.

Obviously, there's no conflict there. If, however, you couldn't care less about providing good service – if you didn't see it as an important part of your job – there *would* be a conflict, and you'd be destined for serious problems and unhappiness down the road.

Bottom line, *every employee* is expected to support, commit to, and act in accordance with your organization's values. And that goes double for you as a leader.

It's extremely rare when good and noble business values aren't shared and embraced by everyone in the workforce. What's critical, however, is to making sure that *shared* values translate into *behaved* values.

The odds are high that you work for an organization whose values are consistent with yours. That makes it much easier to lead by those values because you're merely doing what you believe in. If you find there's a conflict, however, you'll need to work on changing your thinking and behavior – or changing your employer.

LEADING WITH VALUES Lesson

Study your organization's values and determine how they apply to you and the people you lead.

Reflect on your organization's values and your personal values system.
Make sure they're in sync with one another.

Try not to become a person of success,
but rather try to become a person of value.

~ Albert Einstein
(adaptation)

Top 10 Characteristics of Ethical Leaders
and Values-Driven Organizations
Go to www.walkthetalk.com

2 Be A Values Role Model For Your Employees

"**B**e a role model," you say. "That's Mom and Apple Pie stuff." Everyone tells you to do it; no one tells you *how* to do it. This chapter will help change that.

In order to set the proper example, you first need to be committed to the values of your organization, and then you have to practice them – all the time ... without exception.

Bringing values to life is a *behavioral* issue. So you need to put your focus on what you DO day-in and day-out. Obviously, there's a myriad of actions and activities that come into play here. To be a values role model for your employees, you need to pay attention to *everything* you do – because **everything you do COUNTS!** A good starting point is to examine (and consistently monitor) the following four items:

- ■ How you spend your time,
- ■ Where you go;
- ■ What you say;
- ■ How you deal with problems and crises.

How You Spend Your Time

Face it. How you spend your time is the true indicator of what's important to you. No matter what you say, the things to which you give your focus and attention – what you actually DO – are the things that you're really committed to.

Employees aren't dumb. They watch how you spend your time and they conclude: "That's what is important ... that's okay to do ... that's what *we* should do." The opposite is also true. The things that drop off of your peoples' radar screens the fastest are the ones that you ignore. "The boss doesn't spend much time on this anymore. I guess it's really not that important. Maybe it never was."

As a leader, you need to analyze your daily tasks and activities. Are you spending your time doing things that support your organizational values? If yes, congratulations – keep it up! If no, work on adjusting your priorities. Remember that actions speak louder than words.

Like it or not, most of your employees will follow your lead. The primary question you must continually ask yourself: "What examples am I offering for them to follow?"

We judge ourselves by our intentions.
The rest of the world judges us by our actions.

~ Eric Harvey

Time And Role Modeling
A Case Example

Angelo Santisi is a plant manager for a pharmaceutical company that proudly touts "Quality" as one of its organizational values.

Angelo sends weekly e-mails to every colleague and team member who works at his site. He updates them on the week's results: what went well, what problems arose, what the weekly rejection and scrap rates were, and which individuals made noteworthy contributions to maintaining/improving the site's overall quality rating. These continual updates are detailed, specific, and written in Angelo's unique personal style. It's clear that it takes him a few hours to compose them.

By providing these e-mail updates, Angelo both supports and reinforces the company's *Quality* value. The people who work there know that he pays attention to the site's performance and is aware of its successes and problems.

And, by devoting a little of his valuable time to creating and distributing these reports, Angelo sends a clear message to his people about the importance of *Quality* – and demonstrates his commitment to that critically important organizational value.

Where You Go

Most organizations have one or more values that are "inclusive" in nature – recognizing (and communicating) that all employees are valuable and needed members of the workforce. Typically, these values are presented as concepts such as: "Dignity," "Mutual Respect," and "Teamwork." One of the best ways to model these values is to get out of your office (work area) and visit with your people. Nothing shows that you respect employees more than taking the time to interact with them in *their* territory.

Good sales managers know this very well. They spend a meaningful amount of time visiting with their field reps – providing updates, coaching them, observing them, and more importantly, just being there to show support. [It's funny how geographic separation often leads to spending more time with one's employees, and close proximity frequently leads to less time together.]

One manufacturing location I worked with actually mandated that monthly "state of the company" meetings be held so employees could get to know their supervisors and truly feel like part of the team. There's no question that getting out, meeting, and interacting with people is one of the most important jobs a leader can perform.

Even if your organization does not have "inclusive" values, being where the action is allows you to demonstrate the importance you attach to the day-to-day work of your department and the people who do it. You send a powerful message about what you consider important merely by showing up ... and showing an interest.

What You Say

As a leader, you "say" things in a number of different ways. You say things in one-to-one discussions with the people who report to you. You say things in your written communications – both hard copy and e-mail. You say things when you post items on bulletin boards. You say things when you conduct meetings. You say things when you say nothing at all. It's all about communication, and as the saying goes: "You can't *not* communicate."

Whatever you say (or don't say) speaks volumes about your view of organizational values. For example: If your organization says it embraces innovation and creativity but you never ask people if there's a better way of doing things, you end up condoning the status quo. On the other hand, if you tactfully challenge "We've always done it this way" responses and thinking, you demonstrate a commitment to your organization's values.

How You Deal With Problems And Crises

Problems and crises not only present excellent opportunities for you to model your organization's values, they also demonstrate the truth or fiction of your personal commitment *to* those values. In times of stress, people tend to show their "true colors." If you react to problems in a manner consistent with your organization's beliefs and principles, you *and the values* gain credibility with your people. If, however, you react to problems in a manner that's contrary to values, your credibility will be shattered. It's just that plain and simple.

So, the next time you're faced with a problem or crisis, SLOW DOWN. Do your best to remain calm. Ask yourself: "What guidance do our values provide for handling this situation?" Think about the answer for a minute, and then decide what you're going to do.

For many of us, this goes against our grain – we tend to think that problems and crises call for warp-speed action. Well, we must act swiftly and deliberately – but not at the expense of thinking things through. Unfortunately, when all is said and done, decisions made and actions taken in the heat of the moment can undermine your credibility as a leader.

LEADING WITH VALUES Lesson

**Spend your time in a way that
highlights your organization's values.**

**Get out of your office (work area)
and interact with the people who
work with you and for you.**

Watch what you say ... and don't say.

**When things get hot, slow down,
stay calm, and use values as your guide.**

How Ethical Am I?
A Self-Assessment
Go to www.walkthetalk.com

3 Communicate Values As Job Expectations

All good leadership starts with a clear, unambiguous statement of expectations. Leaders must clarify, in specific terms, exactly what it is they expect their employees to do ... how they want and need their people to perform. This applies to things such as work schedules (attendance), sales or production goals and quotas, and values. Yes, values. You can't expect your people to live your organization's values if you don't make it very clear that *everyone* (including you) is accountable for performing in a manner that's consistent with your organization's important beliefs and guiding principles.

Early on, you'll want to teach team members about your values and what practicing them entails. [More about this in the next chapter.] However, the first and most important step you must take is to clearly communicate that demonstrating values-driven performance and business practices is a core part of everyone's job – regardless of his or her level, function, tenure, or geographic location.

However, just *saying* that you expect people to "live" your organization's values doesn't guarantee that they will actually do so. And since all good leaders would prefer that their employees operated from a commitment rather than a mere compliance mode, you may find that you'll need to become a *salesperson* for organizational values.

You may not realize it, but effective leadership involves quite a bit of salesmanship (as opposed to dictatorship).

As a leader, you need to convincingly *sell* your team members on the importance of "being about" what the organization *says* it is about.

Do a good job at that, and employees will bring your business values to life because they *want* to. That will make *your* life easier. You won't have to constantly be looking over people's shoulders – they'll be doing the right things because they understand the reason for doing so.

A word of caution here: Communicating values as expectations – and "selling" people on their importance – should not be geared toward getting everyone to do everything in the exact manner that you would. If that's your agenda, you'll wind up stifling creativity and independent thinking. You need to encourage the kind of innovation where people develop and try new ways of doing things that are consistent with your business values and *add value* to your work processes.

Unquestionably, the best way to convince people that your organization's values are important is for you to make them a priority. Focus your efforts on ensuring that all employees know they are responsible for bringing values to life. Help team members see the importance of doing so. Make it clear that you are paying attention not only to *what* is accomplished, but also *how* it is done.

When living in accordance with the values becomes *your* number one priority, it will become the priority of the people you lead.

LEADING WITH VALUES Lesson

**Employees can't read your mind.
You have to make it very clear
that you expect them to live your
organization's values – and "sell" them
on the importance of doing that.**

*One of the best ways to ensure that values
"happen" is to treat them like work rules.*

~ David Cottrell

The Four Critical Dimensions of
Effective Communication
Go to www.walkthetalk.com

*When I first came to work here,
I was given information on what
our values were.*

*But no one explained why they
were important ... or that making
them happen was part of my job.*

*They must have thought I'd
figure that out by myself.*

~ Anonymous Employee

4 Become A Teacher ... By Asking Questions

In addition to being salespeople, effective leaders are also teachers. They understand that they hold the primary responsibility for helping people understand how values apply to, and guide, daily activities.

While there are literally hundreds of educational techniques one can apply, you'll find that thoughtfully conceived and well-timed questions are great allies of anyone who wants to be an effective teacher.

Properly directed inquiries say a lot about what you consider to be important. Ask thought-provoking questions that pertain to your organization's values and you'll find people will quickly realize that values are important ... and that you take them seriously.

Effective teachers use questions to do three things:

1. Point people in the right direction;
2. Assist in developing critical-thinking skills;
3. Help people articulate what they already know.

You can **point people in the right direction** by asking very simple questions. Here's an example: Sally Simpson is an HR manager for an automotive after-market manufacturer. One of her company's stated values is "teamwork." Sally has prominently displayed a sign in her office that reads WHO ELSE NEEDS TO KNOW? – which is the exact question she asks staff members who bring suggested projects and ideas to her. At first, people were somewhat stumped by that question. However, she persisted. And now, most folks answer it without being asked. By using this simple question, Sally points people in the direction of teamwork ... and they do the rest.

Critical thinking is the ability to assess a situation and determine the appropriate course of action. Critical-thinking skills are essential in today's fast-paced, ever-changing world. You can **develop your staff's critical-thinking skills** through the use of questions. Used properly, questions can assist people in analyzing issues and determining the proper course of action. One of the best questions you can ask a team member who's having trouble deciding what to do is: "What do our values tell you is the right thing to do here?" Once the person answers, you may need to follow up with "What if ..." and "Have you thought of this ..." questions. You'll find that employees will become better thinkers – and they'll soon develop the habit of factoring organizational values into decision-making processes on their own.

The final use of questions is to **assist people in articulating what they already know** intuitively. This type of questioning is particularly useful in helping others gain the confidence they need to be successful.

When one of your people asks for your advice on a subject in which you feel they are competent, turn the tables. Ask: "With our values in mind, what do *you* think we should do?" You'll probably be surprised at how often those same people will come up with good answers by themselves. And when they do, make sure you reinforce them for practicing values-based decision making. If, however, their answers are not in-line with organizational beliefs and principles, ask for alternative suggestions – ones that will better support your values.

LEADING WITH VALUES Lesson

**Merely knowing what your values *are*
is not enough.**

**Values are only words unless, and until,
they are USED to guide behavior ...
and it's every leader's responsibility to
help employees learn to do that.**

*Leading is synonymous with teaching.
Both activities are about the same thing:
showing the way.*

~ Paul Sims

Memorization Versus Meaning
Values Horror Story #2

A large, U.S. based, multinational company decided that developing and communicating a set of core values worldwide was important to its future success. The company was a very strong marketer – known for its clever point-of-sale materials. They approached the job of communicating the core values as they would the launch of a major new product. No expense was spared. There were videos, posters, wallet cards, desk sets, etc. – all emblazoned with the values. By all initial accounts, the "campaign" was a great success.

Several months later, the CEO was touring the sales and marketing offices in one of the overseas locations. As he was passing one of the many cubicles, he noticed that the person working there had a values poster tacked to the wall. Jokingly he said, "Quick, without looking, tell me what our fifth core value is?" The worker jumped to her feet and recited the fifth core value verbatim.

The CEO was impressed. He inquired if everyone at this location was so knowledgeable of the values. The employee said: "Yes, sir. We all know the core values very well. Our manager made us learn them ... he gives us written tests to make sure we know them." Hearing that, the visiting executive said: "That's great! Now, tell me what that value means ... and how it applies to your job." At a loss, the employee responded, "I'm not sure about that ... but I can name all the other values."

The CEO left shaking his head.

5 Remove Obstacles To Bringing Values To Life

Your most important job as a leader is to help your people succeed – and that includes helping them be successful at bringing values to life. Doing that sometimes involves "smoothing the way." Why? Because, unfortunately, *obstacles* to values-driven performance are more common than most managers would like to think. And it's your job to identify those roadblocks, eliminate (or minimize) them whenever possible, and show team members how to deal with those that can't be removed.

When people tell you (or you sense) that they are facing such obstacles – things beyond their control and not of their doing – you must get involved ... you must take the point and show them the way.

29

Obstacles To Living The Values

from *WALK THE TALK ... And Get The Results You Want*
(the best-selling book about bringing values to life)

A sign identified the location of Bill's next learning experience: **The Museum of Corporate Contradictions**. Bill found a two-foot square glass case. Inside the case was a small pedestal that supported one single paper clip. "Where's the display? There's nothing here but a paper clip." "That's it!" replied Clarence. "The paper clip *is* the display. Do you know how many people have to approve buying one carton of those clips and how long it takes to get them? Two. Two people have to approve them, and it takes two weeks to get them. If it's two approvals and two weeks for paper clips, you can imagine what it must be for other things."

The next display item to capture Bill's focus was a red metal case labeled **Supervisor's Tool Box**. Bill unsnapped the latch and lifted the lid. "It's empty!" he exclaimed. "There's nothing in here." "Seems like that could be a big problem," acknowledged Clarence. "If you want to get the job done, you've got to have the right tools. Either you've got them when they hire you, or the company's got to give them to you. But I've seen a lot of supervisors walking around here with empty tool boxes. They're doing the best they can, but they could do a lot better."

These examples really make the point about obstacles. As a leader, you need to make it *easier* for employees to do their jobs. Just as no one should have to wait two weeks to get paper clips, your people shouldn't have to jump through bureaucratic hoops in order to practice the principles that your organization says are important.

Employees are likely to encounter three types of situations that impede their efforts and good intentions. They are identified on the next two pages.

Situation 1

Certain organizational policies and procedures make it difficult for people to engage in values-driven business practices.

Remedy

Address this situation by reviewing your rules and guidelines, and then working to change those that make it difficult for team members to do what you expect them to do.

One leader attacked this all-too-common problem by creating a "Stupid Policy Alert Form." She invited all of her people to identify policies, procedures, and practices that got in the way of doing their jobs effectively and compromised the organization's values. She then began working with senior management to bring about the necessary changes. This one was a "win-win." Her people were happier, operational efficiency improved, and organizational values were enhanced.

Situation 2

People don't realize that they have the wherewithal to remove (or at least overcome) values obstacles.

Remedy

Have employees make a list of the obstacles they face, and work with them to identify the appropriate and expected responses. Clarify how much latitude and discretion team members have in dealing with workplace issues. Encourage everyone to notify you when obstacles present themselves – and recognize employees who do so. Finally, make it clear that some obstacles can't be removed, and that people will not be held accountable – as long as they have made a good-faith effort to do the right thing.

Situation 3

People lack the knowledge, skills, strategies, and techniques necessary to practice certain organizational values.

Remedy

Clarify your expectations, and then help people develop the requisite skills to meet those expectations.

Two factors come into play here: willingness and ability.

Willingness is all about commitment and confidence. Your people need both in order to have the drive and desire to live the organization's values. The example you set, and the guidance you provide, will go a long way toward building team-member commitment and confidence. **Ability**, on the other hand, is about skills. And skills need to be developed and nurtured. The best way to do that is through a combination of coaching, formal classes, mentoring, on-the-job training (OJT), and specific, ongoing feedback.

LEADING WITH VALUES Lesson

Make it easier for your people to live organizational values by removing (or minimizing) any obstacles they face, and by equipping them to handle those barriers that can't be eliminated.

6 Reward Those Who Live The Values

The very best way to ensure that people will continue doing what you want is to give them recognition when they do it. This is especially true when it comes to practicing values.

Reward people for acting in a manner consistent with your organization's values, and you'll find that they'll keep on acting that way. Reward them frequently – by means of specific feedback – and pretty soon you'll have a values-driven workforce.

Most leaders know the two criteria of effective feedback: specificity and timeliness. It's not good enough to merely tell someone that he or she "is doing a great job living the values." Instead, you need to say something like, "I saw you go out of your way to handle Mrs. Williams' problem yesterday. Rather than passing her along to someone else, you got the information she needed. That's an excellent example of living our Customer Service value. I appreciate what you did very much."

A simple statement like that meets both feedback criteria. It's specific because it focuses on what the person did, and it's timely because it is delivered soon after the event took place.

As a leader, it's imperative that you avoid the "I'm not going to reward them for what they're supposed to be doing anyway" trap. [More about that on the next page.] People *crave* recognition. Give it to them. Recognition is one of the few things in this world that is highly valued by the person who receives it and yet costs nothing to the giver. That's an unbelievably good deal! Smart leaders know this, and they actively search out opportunities to compliment and thank employees for doing the right thing.

Recognition is a pretty simple process. Before you meet with the individual, take a minute or two to determine exactly why you want to recognize this person. What did he or she do? Why was it important and valuable? Once you've done this quick preparation, you're ready to meet.

Begin the conversation by saying that you want to compliment the team member for doing something that indicates he or she is living the values. Be specific about what he or she did, identify which value is involved, explain why the contribution is so important (i.e., how it positively impacts the organization), and close with a "Thank You." Then, shut up and listen.

Some people may be embarrassed. Others may merely say "thank you" and go on their way. A few may seize the opportunity to engage you in conversation about something that's on their mind. But here's one you can take to the bank: *All* employees will appreciate the fact that you noticed ... and that you took the time to recognize their efforts.

Gift Versus Strategy
Two Perspectives On Recognition

Sam is a conscientious and dedicated supervisor who – by his own admission – is from the "old school." He has a strong set of beliefs that was forged early in his working career. One of those beliefs has to do with recognition. As Sam sees it, recognition is a *gift* – something special. By his way of thinking, "You don't give people gifts for doing what they're supposed to do ... for just doing their jobs." Go way above and beyond the call of duty, and he will praise you. But merely do what he expects you to do, and you won't hear from Sam – unless, of course, you screw up.

Sam applies this management philosophy to all areas of employee performance and behavior – including the practicing of values. As a result, his people often feel unappreciated (taken for granted). And they're much more concerned about avoiding values violations than they are committed to bringing values to life. The reasons for this are fairly obvious, and the results that Sam gets (or doesn't get) are fairly predictable.

Gloria is a manager who works in the office next to Sam. She's held a leadership position for several years, and she understands a lot about people and their behavior. Unlike Sam, Gloria doesn't view recognition as a gift at all. Instead, she sees it as two things: 1) a "common courtesy" – a way to demonstrate appreciation for employees who make her life easier by doing right, and 2) a "strategy" for getting the performance she wants and needs from her people.

When it comes to the second point, Gloria knows that reinforced behavior is *repeated* behavior. And she uses that knowledge to build a values-driven work unit – and ensure her success as a leader in the process.

Don't read this wrong. Gloria isn't soft on values. Just the opposite – she expects people to abide by the organization's key principles and holds everyone accountable for doing so. But she also looks for, finds, and seizes every opportunity to commend those who meet those expectations. As a result, her team members are motivated to demonstrate their commitment to values every chance they get. In the end, everyone wins – especially Gloria.

LEADING WITH VALUES Lesson

**Recognizing and rewarding behavior
that's in line with your organization's
values is the single best way
to ensure that it continues.**

Always do right by those who DO RIGHT!

~ Al Lucia

Recognition Checklist
Go to www.walkthetalk.com

7 Redirect People Who Aren't Living The Values

Here's where you earn your money as a leader.

It's your job to make sure that all of your team members conduct themselves in a manner consistent with your company's values. In most cases, that isn't too difficult as people will do so willingly. However, you're likely to encounter a few people who just aren't getting with the program – and you need to deal with their behavior. Left unchecked, it can become a problem for your organization and a credibility issue for you.

Just as it's important to recognize people for living the values, it's equally important to hold people who are *not* living the values accountable for changing their behavior.

Seven Reasons Why People Don't Live The Values ... And What To Do About It

1. They don't know *why* the values are important.

Explain the significance of your organization's guiding principles. Make it personal. Use examples that relate specifically to each person and the functions that he or she performs.

2. They don't know *what* they should be doing to live the values.

Teach them what to do. Show them by your example, and cite additional examples of what their colleagues are doing. Help them identify one or two things they can start doing immediately, and monitor their progress.

3. They think values are for other people, not them.

Communicate values as performance expectations. Be clear. Tell employees that you expect *everyone* you lead to live the values. Find out why they think this way. Show them how and why their thinking is misguided.

4. They don't get rewarded for living the values.

Recognize values-driven practices every chance you get. Show your people that *you* notice and appreciate their efforts.

5. They mistakenly think they ARE living the values.

Point out how their behaviors conflict with organizational values. Help them think of alternative actions and decisions that are more values driven.

6. Nothing happens when they DON'T live the values.

Address values violations quickly and deliberately. Take the appropriate action (according to your company policies). Make sure people know the consequences they can expect, and initiate those consequences as necessary.

7. They perceive that living the values is punishing.

Explore their feelings to find out why. Help them reconcile organizational values with their personal values, and remove any obstacles to living the values. Reinforce desired behavior.

This list highlights the most common reasons why people don't live their organization's values. Use it as a guide for dealing with individuals whose behaviors are out of sync with the stated beliefs of your business. Regardless of the reasons for any disconnects, you *will* have to engage your people in meaningful dialogue about the importance of your organizational values, and how their personal behavior is in conflict with one or more of them. And on occasion, disciplinary action may be in order. *That's* the hard part.

Remember, even when you are attempting to change someone's behavior, the key to success is respect. You must show the individual that you respect him or her as a person. Once you establish this, you can address and change the behaviors that are in conflict with your organization's stated beliefs.

Redirecting people who are not living the values is one of the most important things you can do. If you permit employees to engage in improper behavior, your work unit will suffer ... and so will your credibility.

LEADING WITH VALUES Lesson

**Ensure your credibility by
redirecting behavior that is not in line
with your organization's values.**

*Your real performance standards are
not the behaviors you expect, but rather
the behaviors you accept.*

~ Barbara "BJ" Gallagher

8 Never Give In Or Give Up

This final strategy requires little in the way of supporting text – it's pretty much self-explanatory.

As a leader, you must never lose focus of, or compromise the many things that are important to the success of your business. There's a large list of items that you need to pay constant attention to. And at the very top of that list is where you'll find organizational values.

To be sure, every member of your workforce is responsible for values-driven business practices. But ensuring that good intentions translate into actual behavior starts with leadership ... it starts with YOU.

You set the tone for the people in your work group. No matter if the example you provide is good or bad, expect that the vast majority of employees will follow your lead. Take a cavalier approach to values - or lose sight of them altogether – and you give all of your team members license to do the same. But refuse to give in to pressures and obstacles, and your people will have an excellent model to replicate.

41

Summary Flowchart

Develop a personal understanding
of, and commitment to,
your organization's values.

Use this understanding and
commitment to become a values
role model for your people.

Then ask yourself several questions ...

| *Do employees realize that you are holding them accountable for living the values?* | **If *NO*** | Communicate values as expectations. |

| *Do employees know what to DO in order to live your organization's values?* | **If *NO*** | Become a teacher; ask questions; show them how. |

| *Do employees have the clear capacity to live the organization's values?* | **If *NO*** | Minimize/remove the obstacles, or help people work around them. |

| *Do employees experience positive consequences for values-driven behavior?* | **If *NO*** | Provide recognition to employees who bring the organization's values to life. |

| *Do employees experience negative consequences for NOT living the values?* | **If *NO*** | Redirect team members who are out of sync with organizational beliefs and principles. |

Closing Thoughts

So there you have it ... there you have *them* – eight simple, common-sense, and proven strategies for LEADING WITH VALUES.

Follow the guidelines found on the previous pages, and watch your organization flourish as its values come alive for (and by) your people. Ignore them, and watch those same values decrease in meaning and importance until they're not worth much more than the paper they're typically written on.

As Eric Harvey and Al Lucia say in *WALK THE TALK ... And Get The Results You Want,* "Values are the gold in each of us – they're the real fortune of any organization." Don't let *your* organization's fortune sit around gathering dust. Instead, use it to help you realize bigger and better things. That is, after all, your responsibility as a leader. And to meet that responsibility, you must put your initial focus on the person you see in the mirror.

Make sure you understand how organizational values relate to *you* as well as the people you lead. Set the example by ensuring that *your* behavior is in sync with those guiding principles at all times. Know the way, show the way, and GO the way. By doing that, you will have "earned the right" to insist that others do the same.

Next, make sure your people know that you are holding them (and yourself) accountable for living your organization's values. Use questions to teach them how to apply values to their decisions and daily activities. Make it easier for them to live the values by minimizing any obstacles they face. And by all means, make sure you recognize individuals who are values-driven and redirect those who get off course.

Finally, never give up. Persistence is key for LEADING WITH VALUES. Despite our best intentions, most of us aren't in sync with our *personal* values one-hundred percent of the time. The same is true for *organizational* values. Fact is, we're all human. *You* will experience occasional values slips – and so will your people. But being human is a condition, not an excuse. The key is persistence.

Together, these eight strategies form a blueprint for building and maintaining a values-driven organization. Learn them, practice them, continually improve on your use of them, and you'll shape a powerhouse organization capable of achieving anything it sets out to do.

To be sure, these strategies are not rocket science. But there is a touch of genius in them. And as the old adage goes, "Genius is nothing more than elegant common sense." Ignore these practices at your own risk. Or be a genius and use them – and watch your organization grow and prosper.

LEAD ON ... WITH VALUES.

The Walk The Talk Company

Since 1977, **The WALK THE TALK Company** has helped individuals and organizations, worldwide, achieve success through Values-Based Practices. Our goal is both simple and straightforward: **to provide you and your organization with high-impact resources for your personal and professional success!**

We specialize in ...
- "How-To" Handbooks and Support Material
- Group Training Programs
- Inspirational Gift Books and Movies
- Do-It-Yourself Training Resources
- Motivational Newsletters
- 360° Feedback Processes
- The Popular *Start Right...Stay Right* and *Santa's Leadership Secrets*® Product Lines
- *And much more*!

The Author

An internationally respected speaker, consultant, executive coach, and author, **Bud Bilanich** is well known for his business common sense. He brings a straightforward, no-nonsense approach to his work of enhancing the performance of individuals, teams, and organizations.

In today's uncertain and challenging business environment, Bud's domestic and international clients report that his back-to-basics, real-world advice is just what they need to solve their tough business problems.

Bud is a sought after, engaging, and entertaining keynote speaker. Audiences worldwide have acclaimed his unique ability to simplify complex topics and present them in a down-to-earth, useful way.

Visit

WALKTHETALK.COM

Resources for Personal and Professional Success

To Learn More

Leadership and Employee Development Center

- Develop your Leaders
- Build Employee Commitment
- Achieve Business Results

Free Newsletters

- Daily Inspiration
- The Power of Inspiration
- The Leadership Solution

Motivational Gift Books

- Inspire your Team
- Create Customer Enthusiasm
- Reinforce Core Values

Additional Leadership Development Resources

The Leadership Secrets of Santa Claus – A "sack full" of contents to include Santa's Eight Secrets for getting big things done in your workshop ... all year long. – $14.95

Monday Morning Leadership – A powerful guide on how to be a mentor, coach, and become a highly skilled "people developer." – $14.95

144 Ways to Walk the Talk – A quick reference handbook packed with 144 proven leadership techniques to help build a high performance culture and results-oriented team. – $10.95

Ethics4Everyone – The handbook and "how to" guide to ensure ethical behaviors and integrity-based business practices. – $10.95

Lead Right – Collection of ideas and proven strategies guaranteed to help you become a more effective and respected leader.– $12.95

***Nuts'nBolts* Leadership** – Provides proven, practical, and easy to follow tips to energize employees and build commitment to the organization's mission. – $10.95

Listen UP, Leader! – Provides powerful insights into what employees want and the seven characteristics of leadership that people will follow. – $10.95

The Manager's Coaching Handbook – A "cut to the chase" practical guide to confronting and improving the performance of your "super stars, middle stars, and falling stars." – $10.95

Ethics & Values Alignment Training

The WALK THE TALK Success Series – The award-winning video training package based on the bestselling book *WALK THE TALK ... And Get The Results You Want.* – $875.00

   ✓ 30-minute VHS
   ✓ Step-by-step leader's guide
   ✓ Three powerful WALK THE TALK resources

Ethics4Everyone – A complete training package designed to teach ethics awareness and skills to employees at ALL levels. – $995.00

       ✓ VHS/DVD with 14-minute main show and 10-minute bonus leadership segment
       ✓ PowerPoint® presentation on CD-ROM
       ✓ Ten sets of participant materials

To preview these training resources, *please call* **1.888.822.9255**

Please send me additional copies of LEADING WITH VALUES

1-99 copies: $10.95 ea.   100-499 copies: $9.95 ea.   500+ copies: *please call*

LEADING WITH VALUES _____ copies X _____ = $_____

Additional Leadership Development Resources

The Leadership Secrets of Santa Claus	_____ copies X	$ 14.95 = $_____	
Monday Morning Leadership	_____ copies X	$ 14.95 = $_____	
144 Ways To Walk The Talk	_____ copies X	$ 10.95 = $_____	
Ethics4Everyone	_____ copies X	$ 10.95 = $_____	
Lead Right	_____ copies X	$ 14.95 = $_____	
Nuts 'nBolts Leadership	_____ copies X	$ 10.95 = $_____	
Listen UP, Leader!	_____ copies X	$ 10.95 = $_____	
The Manager's Coaching Handbook	_____ copies X	$ 10.95 = $_____	

Product Total $_____

*Shipping & Handling $_____

Subtotal $_____

Sales Tax:

(Sales Tax Collected on TX Customers Only)

Texas Sales Tax – 8.25% $_____

Total (U.S. Dollars Only) $_____

---

*Shipping and Handling Charges
For actual shipping rates, please visit WalktheTalk.com

Name_____ Title_____

Organization_____

Shipping Address_____

City_____ State_____ Zip _____

Phone_____ Fax_____
(No P.O. Boxes)

E-Mail_____

Charge Your Order: ☐ MasterCard   ☐ Visa   ☐ American Express

Credit Card Number_____ Exp. Date_____

☐ Check Enclosed (Payable to: The WALK THE TALK Company)

☐ Please Invoice (**Orders over $250 ONLY**) P. O. Number (if required)_____

WALKTHETALK.COM
Resources for Personal and Professional Success

PHONE 1.888.822.9255 or 972.899.8300 M-F, 8:30-5:00 Cen.	**ON-LINE** www.walkthetalk.com	**MAIL** WalkTheTalk.com 1100 Parker Square, Suite 250 Flower Mound, TX 75028
	FAX 972.899.9291	

Prices effective October 2012 are subject to change.